Brad Lakin

I0473908

11 MISTAKES
Car Accident Injury Victims Make

by

Brad Lakin

Attorney at Law

Cover design by Kris Lakin

Published by Dominate Media LLC

Brad Lakin

Brad Lakin

CONTENTS

11 Mistakes Car Accident Injury Victims Make

About the Author

Brad Lakin, Esq. is a best-selling author who has been inducted in the National Academy of Best Selling Authors and a trial lawyer who is often sought out by media to discuss his clients' cases. Brad has appeared on ABC, CBS, NBC, FOX affiliates, and CNN, and has been quoted and highlighted in newspapers throughout the country.

Brad has repeatedly been recognized by his peers as a Super Lawyer, a Rising Star, one of America's Premier Experts® and in 2006 as one of Forty Lawyers Under Forty to Watch. He has also been honored as a Top 100 Trial Lawyer by the National Trial Lawyers, a nationwide organization.

These honors stem from his success as a litigator in the courtroom.

In a 2005 product liability trial, Lakin helped his clients win a $43 million victory – the second largest verdict in Illinois and the 30th nationwide. The case was a featured story throughout the country and included an appearance on CNN's Anderson Cooper 360.

Brad has tried cases to verdict in Illinois, Oklahoma, Arkansas, West Virginia, Nebraska, Missouri, and Ohio. During the course of his career, his firms have represented clients in all 50 states.

Brad's passion for nursing home abuse cases stems from a personal tragedy that happened to a member of his family. Brad's goal in his work and for this book is to prevent the same type of tragedy from happening to others. Brad is known nationally for his successful courtroom advocacy in personal injury, mass torts, and a variety of complex litigation matters. His firm has recovered over $700

million in verdicts, settlements, and benefits for
their clients. To learn more about Brad Lakin and
his firm, visit www.GreatInjuryLawyers.com or call
(800) 550-2106.

1) FAILING TO REPORT THE ACCIDENT TO THE POLICE

There are two very important reasons why you must file a police report. First, most state laws require a police report. Most people are not aware that an accident report is required by law when one of the following occurs: property damage over a certain value, personal injury or death.

As a matter of fact, in some states failing to report the accident can subject the driver to a fine. Second, it's the best way for you to document the facts and circumstances of your car crash. Both are vitally important for your property damage claim and/or a personal injury claim.

By reporting the wreck to the local police, who fill out a police report, the facts and circumstances of the incident are made official and provide support for any claim that you may be required to make in the future.   Many don't feel an accident report is necessary because they don't think they're injured.

This is a common mistake people make. People believe they're not injured only to wake up the next morning and learn otherwise. By contacting the police and filling out an accident report you've made "the wreck" an official government record. In doing so, the other driver/s can never deny the wreck happened.

2) FAILING TO PROMPTLY NOTIFY THE INSURANCE COMPANY

Insurance companies treat claims promptly reported differently. Later reported claims are met with a greater scrutiny than those reported within a reasonable time. You should promptly report your wreck to your insurance carrier. Most policies have a language in the policy requiring you to notify your insurance carrier.

When you contact the insurance company be prepared to give a short explanation as to how the accident occurred and any symptoms of injury you are experiencing. This should be a short concise explanation. At this stage, you should _not_ give a recorded statement to your insurance company or the insurance company for the faulty driver.

You should seek out legal advice from a qualified car accident attorney before giving a statement to your own insurance company or the at fault driver's insurance carrier.

Be prepared to provide the insurance company with:

a) The date of incident

b) The location of the incident

c) The names of others involved in the wreck

d) The names of anyone who claims to have witnessed the wreck; and a copy of the police report, if you have a copy.

3) FAILING TO SEEK PROMPT MEDICAL ATTENTION

In an auto case, the victim or the injured person always has the responsibility of proving negligence in order to recover money damages for their injuries. If you don't seek immediate medical attention, you undermine or otherwise hurt your chances of recovering fair compensation for your injuries. Understandably, most people wish to take a "wait and see how I feel" approach.

But this can be a huge mistake. Why? Because with every hour or day that you delay seeking medical attention, you lend support to the insurance company adjuster's or lawyer's argument that you must have injured yourself doing something else (i.e. housework or mowing the grass). Or, they argue that you must not be injured too badly because you didn't to seek immediate medical attention.

It's very important for you not to ignore the immediate signs and symptoms of an injury, even if they seem minor at the time. You should see a doctor immediately to avoid these common pitfalls. Best case scenario, you see a doctor for symptoms that go away.

4) FAILING TO UNDERSTAND WHO PAYS FOR THE DAMAGE TO YOUR CAR

As is the case with an injury claim, the at fault driver will be responsible for paying the damage to your car. You should get a couple of estimates from local reputable auto shops. A good auto shop will help you with your insurance issues. You have two alternatives. First, submit your claim to the at fault driver's insurance company.

They will either pay to your satisfaction or not. Alternatively, you can submit it to your own insurance company provided you have the appropriate coverage. You may be reluctant to do this because you have to pay a deductible. If you submit the claim to your own company they will negotiate, and if necessary arbitrate, with the at fault driver's insurance company and pay your deductible back, if successful. This normally takes between 1-6 months.

How much are you paid? Most policies provide payment for the costs to "repair or replace" your damaged car or the "actual cash value of the car," whichever is less. In other words, if the cost to repair is greater than the value of your car, the insurance company will declare it a "total" and pay you accordingly.

Make sure you get fair value and do your own research via sources like Kelly Blue Book (www.kbb.com). If your vehicle is "totaled," you may negotiate with the insurance company regarding the actual cash value. Don't simply accept their first offer if you feel it's not fair.

5) GIVING THE INSURANCE COMPANY A STATEMENT

This can be DEVASTATING. In your dealings with the insurance adjusters, whether your own company or the at fault driver's company, always be polite and courteous. They are human and will be most responsive and helpful to those who are friendly. Most insurance companies or insurance adjusters will leave you with the impression that you're either required to give a statement or it is necessary in order to process your claim. Neither is accurate. If asked to give a statement simply say something like:

a) "I'm not feeling well and do not wish to give a statement at this time."

b) "It's my understanding that I'm not required to give a statement and right now I prefer to not give formal statement."

c) "At the appropriate time I'll give you a statement

but right now I prefer not to."

There are various reasons why you shouldn't give a statement to the insurance companies. First, it's the insurance adjuster's job to protect the best interest of the insurance company. That means saving the insurance company money. It doesn't mean they are bad people. Bottom line, his or her interest is not aligned with your interest.

Second, you may unintentionally leave out vital information, or fail to explain <u>all</u> the reasons why the other driver was a fault, that can later be used against you should a dispute regarding your claim arise. Third, timing is everything. An accident is an emotionally and physically traumatic event, which can affect the way you explain matters.

Both leave the insurance company with ammunition to argue that you were less than truthful about your claim. I can't tell you the number of times that clients have given statements but later say "that's not exactly how it happened," "I forgot to tell them about X" or "they twisted my words." Please talk to a qualified personal injury attorney, in advance, if you're inclined to give a statement.

6) FAILING TO GIVE A DETAILED MEDICAL HISTORY TO YOUR MEDICAL PROVIDERS

When you first see your doctor, or other providers like a physical therapist, it's very important that you provide information regarding:

a) Past injuries or illnesses

b) A history of how your accident occurred

c) Your complications, if any.

It's best, if the circumstances permit, to write down this information prior to your doctor's visit. This is important for three reasons. First, if you fail to give your physician a thorough explanation of your past medical history, the insurance company will later argue that you've been less than honest or intentionally left out important medical information. This is EXTREMELY important if you had a prior injury to the same area of the body.

Second, explaining how the accident occurred is important to establish the following: the mechanism of your injury and to help your doctor analyze whether your injury was related to your auto wreck.

Third, you should give a detailed explanation about the symptoms and problems you're experiencing. Explain specifically what areas of the body are being affected and what kind of pain it is producing. It's best to think about this information in advance of your appointment, if able, so you don't leave anything out.

7) ALLOWING THE INSURANCE COMPANY TO DRIVE A WEDGE BETWEEN YOU AND YOUR DOCTOR

A few simple steps can prevent a lot of headaches. The physician patient relationship can be damaged when your doctor's bills are either denied or not paid promptly. Insurance companies know this and often drag their feet or deny claims. The at fault driver will ultimately be responsible for your medical bills with any settlement.

But, his or her insurance carrier is not required to pay your medical bills immediately following a car accident. It's a total waste of time to try to pursue the at fault driver's insurance company for these expenses. This will only occur at the end of the process when your claim is finally resolved.

There are two basic steps to avoid this common pitfall and keep your medical provider happy.

Brad Lakin

If you have medical insurance, simply ask your medical provider to bill the group health insurance provider. You should also provide your medical provider with your own auto insurance company's information for billing under your Medical Payments Coverage. This is a small policy on your auto insurance that's designed to allow you to seek prompt medical attention knowing you'll receive payment.

Keep in mind that this coverage has limits that typically range from $2,000 - $10,000. Just look on your insurance card or declaration sheet to determine your limits. If you later receive a settlement from the at fault driver, the insurance companies may later be entitled to what's referred to as a right of subrogation, if permitted under the policy.

This means the insurance company may be entitled to the right of repayment for the monies it paid your medical providers when you settle with the at fault driver.

These steps will go far in keeping your medical provider happy which will help with his or her willingness to cooperate with your continued treatment and claim. In most situations, your medical provider will do the billing for you provided you give them the necessary information.

8) CANCELLING OR BEING A "NO SHOW" FOR DOCTORS APPOINTMENTS

This can have a negative impact on your injury claim. There's no doubt that life is hectic and you inevitably have good reasons for canceling from time to time. But, you must understand that those reasons are rarely documented in the medical records. If you frequently cancel your doctors appointment, your physician will become irritated and less cooperative with injury claim process. An unhappy doctor makes for a poor witness on your behalf.

Likewise, canceling your appointments will leave the insurance company, the insurance companies adjusters and their lawyers with the wrong impression - your injuries are not that severe or you would have kept your appointments. Do your best to keep all your doctors appointments.

9) UNDERSTATING YOUR MEDICAL COMPLICATIONS TO YOUR MEDICAL PROVIDERS

It's your job to inform your doctor about the exact complications and pain you're experiencing. Keep in mind that your doctor sees many patients each day.   Don't understate, or overstate for that matter, your complications or pain.

Doing so will give the insurance company and its lawyers the ability to successfully argue that you did not have immediate pain so your complications or injuries are not severe or you must have been caused by something other than the wreck. Explain how your pain an complications are affecting your daily activities, work, family and hobbies.

Make sure you are 100% truthful in relating your symptoms to your doctor. This is crucial because the insurance company will be reviewing your medical records at a later date looking for inconsistencies or ammunition to argue you're not being honest or over exaggerating. Do not be concerned that you're complaining about the same issues over and over to your doctor. In fact, documenting this in your medical records for the insurance company and its lawyers is important for them to see how the wreck has impacted you.

10) DISCUSSING YOUR LAWSUIT WITH YOUR DOCTOR

You should not discuss the fact that you are contemplating a potential lawsuit with anyone, let alone your doctor. Yes, this means not posting about it on Facebook! All your Facebook postings will be available to the other side if litigation becomes necessary, even if your profile is "private." Most physicians are only interested in providing you medical care and are not concerned about any legal claim. This information should only be shared with your doctor if he or she asks.

Most doctors prefer not to be involved in lawsuits. If you discuss your lawsuit with your doctor, or that you're thinking about a lawsuit, you may the doctor with the wrong impression. You're more interested in the money from the lawsuit then you are with your own health and well-being.

Your doctor will be less likely to help with your ongoing medical treatment, and ultimately with opinions regarding your care and treatment. It's best not to discuss your lawsuit with your doctor or any one else for that matter.

11) FAILING TO FOLLOW DOCTOR'S ORDERS

It's very important you follow your doctor's recommendations with regard to the following:

a) Medications prescribed

b) Therapy

c) Restrictions

d) Treatment for any psychological problems caused by your injury

e) Any other recommendations.

You should do everything that your doctor asks of you. It's key for two reasons. One, your doctor made these recommendations that he or she believes is in your best well-being. If you fail to follow these recommendations, you spoon feed the insurance company the insurance company adjuster or the insurance company lawyer with information to suggest that your failure to follow the doctor's recommendations is the reason who haven't healed or that you have in fact fully recovered.

Second, by following your doctor's recommendations, he or she becomes an advocate for you during the litigation. A doctor likes to be in a position of telling people "he/she has done everything I've asked." This makes it easier for the doctor to form opinions about your injuries and stick by them under fire from the insurance company and their lawyers.

We hope you found this book to be a valuable resource. We invite your to visit our website at www.GreatInjuryLawyers.com where we've created numerous additional free books, special reports and resources for you.